ANDREW MARVELL

from a miniature by FRANZ CLEYN *reproduced by permission of His Grace the Duke of Buccleuch*

ANDREW MARVELL

by

JOHN PRESS

PUBLISHED FOR
THE BRITISH COUNCIL
BY LONGMAN GROUP LTD

LONGMAN GROUP LTD
Longman House, Burnt Mill, Harlow, Essex

*Associated companies, branches and
representatives throughout the world*

*First published 1958
Revised editions 1966, 1977*
First and revised editions © John Press, 1958, 1966, 1977

*Filmset by Butler & Tanner Ltd
Frome and London
Printed in England by
Bradleys, Reading and London*

ISBN 0 582 01098 5

¶ ANDREW MARVELL was born on 31 March 1621 at Winestead in Holderness, Yorkshire. He died on 16 August 1678, and was buried at St Giles in the Fields, London.

ANDREW MARVELL

I

WHEN Andrew Marvell died in 1678 his admirers mourned him as a verse satirist and pamphleteer whose attacks on the Court and on the pretensions of the Anglican episcopate had made him obnoxious to the government of Charles II. Nowadays he is admired chiefly for a few poems (none of which was published in his lifetime), whose peculiar distinction has been celebrated by T. S. Eliot and by many lesser critics of the past fifty years. We may find it strange that one man should have acquired two such divergent reputations—the first depicting him as a violent, audacious satirist, the second emphasizing the fineness of his lyrical sensibility and the urban, civilized quality of his metaphysical wit.

All modern commentators agree that in his finest poems there is a sense of underlying conflict and tension, although it is not easy to explain its origin. The Civil War and the general political uncertainties of the time may lie at the root of the matter, or it may be that Marvell was profoundly affected by a conflict which was not, in the narrow sense of the word, political—a conflict engendered by the rival claims upon his nature of sensuous Renaissance mysticism, scientific rationalism, and thoughtful, strenuous Puritanism. A study of his life and of his works may illustrate the ways in which Marvell responded to the pressure of public events and to the promptings of his temperament.

II

Andrew Marvell's father, also named Andrew, was an Anglican clergyman strongly influenced by Calvinist doctrine, who in 1624 became 'Lecturer' of Holy Trinity Church, Hull, and Master of the Charterhouse. His home was in the rural parts just outside the bustle of the town, so Andrew Marvell the Younger, who was born at Winestead in Holderness, near Hull, on 31 March 1621, grew up among the sounds and sights and smells of the countryside. Despite Parker's gibe half a century later that Marvell was reared 'among Boatswains and Cabin-boys', it seems probable that he was educated at Hull Grammar School, from where, in 1633, he went up to Cambridge as a Scholar of Trinity College. After going down from Cambridge some time before September 1641, without taking his MA degree, Marvell spent four years travelling on the continent (probably 1642–6), acquiring in the process a knowledge of foreign languages to which Milton testified in 1653.

The elegies of 1648 and 1649 on Villiers, Hastings and Lovelace suggest that, until then, Marvell's sympathies were with the Royalists, although he seems to have taken no active part in the Civil Wars. Nor can we tell why or even when he became converted to the Puritan cause. He may have been repelled by the raffish elements in the Cavalier party and have come to admire the exhilarating virtues of Puritanism, the moral strength and probity which it fostered, its concern for spiritual values and its contempt for worldliness. Yet the stages of his conversion remain a matter of conjecture for, however we may interpret 'An Horatian Ode', there is no satisfactory explanation of the poem which he composed on Tom May's death. May was a former Royalist poet whose desertion to the other side was regarded by his old colleagues as the act of a renegade. We can account for Marvell's hostile references to May by supposing that he personally disliked the dead man; but we can put no such gloss upon his insulting references to the Parliamentary commanders. May died on 13 November 1650: late in 1650 or early in 1651 Marvell was installed at Nunappleton House, Yorkshire, as tutor to Mary Fairfax, daughter of the leading Cromwellian general who had resigned from the army after disagreeing with Cromwell's aggressive policy towards the Scots.

He left Nunappleton late in 1652 or early in the next year, as we know from a letter written by Milton on 21 February 1653 to Bradshaw, President of the Council of State, recommending Marvell's employment as an Assistant Latin Secretary. Although he was not appointed, Marvell was chosen to write the Latin verses which were sent with Cromwell's portrait to Queen Christina of Sweden in April 1654. Having failed to get an official post, Marvell again became a tutor, this time to William Dutton, a ward of Oliver Cromwell's, who lived in John Oxenbridge's household at Eton. In the summer of 1656, William Dutton was in Saumur, accompanied by his tutor, whom J. Scudamore in a letter to Sir Richard Browne, dated 15 August 1656, described as 'one Mervill, a notable English Italo-Machavillian'. Milton's letter to Oldenburg, of 1 August 1657, mentions a learned friend who in the summer of 1656 had lent a copy of Milton's pamphlet against Morus to various scholars in Saumur. The chances are that the learned friend was Andrew Marvell and that he remained at Eton until, on 2 September 1657, he obtained the post in the civil service for which he had applied some years previously. Although in 1673 Marvell claimed that he had 'not the remotest relation to publick matters, nor correspondence with the persons then predominant, until the year 1657', and that he had accepted his appointment with reluctance, the evidence suggests that he welcomed the chance of serving Cromwell, whom he had come to revere as the sole guarantor of peace at home and prestige abroad. His 'Poem upon the death of O.C.', which was not printed until 1681, is more than a eulogy of a dead statesman: the mark of personal grief is stamped upon those lines where Marvell describes how he gazed at Cromwell's body:

> I saw him dead, a leaden slumber lyes,
> And mortal sleep over those wakefull eyes:
> Those gentle rays under the lids were fled,
> Which through his looks that piercing sweetnesse shed;
> That port which so majestique was and strong,
> Loose and depriv'd of vigour, stretch'd along.
>
> (247–52)

In the period of uncertainty after Cromwell's death on 3 September 1658, Marvell began to play an active part in political life, being elected in 1659 as a Member of Parliament for Kingston-upon-Hull, which he continued to represent in the House of Commons until his death in 1678. He probably frequented Harrington's Rota, or political debating club, whose members included the most daring revolutionary thinkers of the time. General Monk's brief dictatorship,

7

followed by the Restoration of Charles II to the throne, compelled the Rota to disperse and marked the end of Harrington's visionary republicanism.

Unlike his fellow-servants of the Commonwealth, Dryden and Waller, Marvell did not write an effusive poem in honour of Charles II, yet despite his obdurate silence and his past record he was not only unpunished but even sent on a diplomatic mission to Holland and on a similar mission to Russia, Sweden and Denmark. His mounting hostility to the policy of Charles II; his speeches in the Commons; his suspected authorship of satires against the Government; the belief that he acted as secretary to Opposition groups who met in coffee-houses (rather as the Rota had once met): all these factors brought him into official disfavour. By 1673, when both parts of *The Rehearsal Transpros'd* had appeared, Marvell was recognized as perhaps the most formidable pamphleteer and satirist of the Opposition, and from 1672–4 he may have worked with Peter Du Moulin, who, as an agent of William of Orange, was trying to break Charles II's alliance with Louis XIV against the Dutch. In the last few years of his life his detestation of the Court became so violent and bitter that he grew increasingly savage and even fanatical in his onslaughts upon his political foes. It is not surprising that he was both dreaded and hated, nor that popular rumour attributed his death to poison, although it is highly probable that he died of tertian fever through lack of proper medical care. He was buried on 18 August 1678, in St Giles in the Fields, London.

III

Friends and enemies of Marvell have left us vivid though all too brief accounts of his character, which we can supplement by fragments of his biography. John Aubrey says of him:

He was a great master of the Latin tongue; an excellent poet in Latin or English: for Latin verses there was no man could come into competition with him.... He was of a middling stature, pretty strong sett, roundish faced, cherry-cheek't, hazell eie,

8

browne haire. He was in his conversation very modest, and of very few words: and though he loved wine he would never drinke hard in company, and was wont to say that, *he would not play the good-fellow in any man's company in whose hands he would not trust his life.* He kept bottles of wine at his lodgeing, and many times he would drinke liberally by himselfe to refresh his spirits, and exalt his muse.

Aubrey remarks that Marvell 'had not a generall acquaintance', but he chose his friends with a discriminating care. Among them were numbered John Pell, a mathematician and a friend of Hobbes; the poet Lovelace; religious and political thinkers such as John Hales and Harrington. His admiration for the satires of Rochester and for Butler's *Hudibras* is a sign that his Puritanism was in no way fanatical or narrow. It was, however, John Milton whom Marvell revered above all his contemporaries. Having, with characteristic loyalty and courage, protected Milton in 1660 from the attacks of his enemies, he continued to defend his conduct and to extol his memory. In the lines 'On Mr Milton's Paradise Lost', printed in the second edition of Milton's poem (1674), he celebrated the genius of his dead friend:

> At once delight and horrour on us seize,
> Thou singst with so much gravity and ease;
> And above humane flight dost soar aloft,
> With Plume so strong, so equal, and so soft.
> The *Bird* nam'd from that *Paradise* you sing
> So never Flags, but alwaies keeps on Wing
>
> (35–40)

Yet if Marvell was a loyal friend he was also a fierce hater, as the virulence of his satirical writings may suggest. He was also a quick-tempered man: we know of three instances in which he began a quarrel that ended in blows, although one of them may have been a playful scuffle. His satires gained him a number of bitter enemies, who jeered at his fashionable manners, his full-bottomed wig, his fondness for larding his conversation with Gallic phrases, and his frequenting of coffee-houses. Not content with these minor insults, they descended to the most scurrilous and extravagant libels, accusing Marvell of having committed homosexual acts with

9

Milton, and suggesting that he had grown virtuous of late only because he had become impotent. The anonymous *A Letter from Amsterdam to a Friend in England* (1678) gets in one or two jabs at Marvell:

... make sure of Andrew; he's a shrewd man against popery, though for his religion you may place him, as Pasquin at Rome placed Henry the Eighth, betwixt Moses, the Messiah and Mahomet, with his motto in his mouth *Quo me vertam nescio*. It is well he is now transposed into politicks; they say he had much ado to live upon poetry.

This last sentence may remind us that, with the publication of *The Rehearsal Transpros'd* (Parts I and II) in 1672 and 1673 Marvell had become famous as a deadly pamphleteer. Samuel Parker had, in his youth, been a Puritan but on becoming an orthodox Anglican soon after the Restoration he did not hesitate to attack and to ridicule his old friends. By 1672, when he was Archdeacon of Canterbury, he had acquired a reputation as a controversialist skilled in defending the Anglican Church against the doctrines of Hobbes and the errors of Protestant Dissenters. He objected to Charles II's Declaration of Indulgence on the grounds that it was unsafe to grant toleration to Roman Catholics or to Protestant rebels against the Anglican hierarchy. In his answer to Parker, Marvell christens his adversary Mr Bayes. The Duke of Buckingham's play, *The Rehearsal*, contains a character named Bayes, who is a malicious caricature of Dryden; Marvell's borrowing from Buckingham enables him both to ridicule Parker and to show his contempt for Dryden. We cannot hope to summarize Marvell's arguments, but we can show why, in Bishop Burnett's words, he had 'all the *laughers* of his side'.

Marvell raises a number of laughs by what present-day readers would regard as dirty abuse, and by sly innuendoes about Parker's keeping a mistress whom Marvell nicknames his 'comfortable Importance'. Even Parker's wife, whom he had married in the interval between the publication of Parts I and II, becomes a target for these indecent jokes. More justifiably, Marvell emphasizes his contempt for a man who had changed sides in order to gain preferment, and who had purged himself of all Puritanical taint by imitating the vices of fashionable society:

> In order to do this he daily enlarged, not only his conversation, but his conscience, and was made free of some of the town-vices; imagining, like Muleasses King of Tunis ... that by hiding himself among the onions, he should escape being traced by his perfumes.

Having drawn attention to Parker's time-serving, Marvell proceeds to expose the weakness of his arguments. Like all dutiful Anglicans, Parker was bound to acknowledge the authority of the King as a temporal sovereign and also as Supreme Governor of the Church of England, yet here he was trying to compel Charles II to persecute the Dissenters. Marvell takes a malicious delight in showing that Anglican loyalty to the Crown will last only as long as the Crown humours the Church's itch to harry its religious opponents:

> Is this at last all the business why he hath been building up all this while the Necessary, Universal, Uncontroulable, Indispensible, Unlimited, Absolute Power of Governors; only to gratifie the humour and arrogance of an Unnecessary, Universal, Uncontroulable, Dispensible, Unlimited and Absolute, Archdeacon? Still must, must, must: But what if the Supream Magistrate won't?

Parker's narrowness and distortion of all sane values invite Marvell's ironical commendation:

> The Church of England is much obliged to Mr *Bayes* for having proved that Nonconformity is the Sin against the Holy Ghost.

He strikes a deeper note when he proclaims the sanctity of the individual conscience, a theme dear to him. Believing that 'the Supreme Magistrate hath some power, but not all Power in matters of Religion', Marvell judges it good morals and sound policy that the ruler should not peer too closely into men's souls, but allow decent, quiet citizens to worship God as they think fit. Parker, who argued that, in religious matters, a subject should be obedient, even against his conscience, was rash enough to advise the subject to say 'My

Obedience will hallow, or at least excuse my Action'. Marvell, with his unfailing verbal dexterity, seizes on this unhappy choice of words:

If ever our Author come for his merits in election to be a Bishop, a man might almost adventure instead of Consecrated to say that he was Excused.

Marvell's prophecy was fulfilled. Parker was consecrated (or excused) Bishop of Oxford in 1687 and characteristically allowed James II to install him as President of Magdalen College, Oxford, in the course of the King's attempt to coerce the University. He lived to enjoy the fruits of his servility and of his Bishopric until 1688.

No other prose work brought Marvell such renown as *The Rehearsal Transpros'd*, although *An Account of the Growth of Popery and Arbitrary Government* (1677), in which he unblushingly attacks Charles II for having issued the Declaration of Indulgence, devastatingly analyses the Government's misdeeds. The *Mock Speech from the Throne* (1675), a masterpiece of cool, bantering irony, has not been proved to be by him, but it is hard not to accept the view of the *doyen* of Marvell scholars, Pierre Legouis, that it comes from Marvell's pen. Modern readers, discerning in this pasquinade those qualities of wit, poise and elegance which they prize in Marvell's verse, will probably value it more highly than all the long political and religious tracts on which he lavished his talents in the closing years of his life.

IV

The *Miscellaneous Poems* of Andrew Marvell appeared in 1681, with a preface by Mary Marvell, assuring the reader that the poems 'are Printed according to the exact copies of my late Dear Husband'. Mary Palmer, for many years Marvell's housekeeper, asserted in the course of the long, sordid law-suit which followed his death that he had secretly married her on or about 13 May 1667 in the Church of the Holy Trinity in the Little Minories, a statement that is hard to disprove since, although all the other church records are intact, the registers of marriage for the years 1662–83 are missing. It seems likely that she arranged for the publication of Marvell's poems to bolster up her extremely shaky claim, and that many purchasers of this volume bought it for the sake of his portrait, which has been torn out of a large number of the surviving copies. Marvell was admired by his contemporaries almost exclusively for his prose, and his poetry remained largely unknown throughout the eighteenth century, despite the publication in 1776 of Thompson's splendid three-volume edition, which seems to have been welcomed chiefly by the Whigs as a weapon in their campaign against George III. Marvell in his *Account of the Growth of Popery* (1677) had used the phrase 'the Country Party' in a sense which, according to the New English Dictionary, it did not acquire until 1735–8. The Whigs of George III's reign, who liked to imagine themselves as the true heirs of the Opposition to Charles II, admired Marvell for what they held to be his republican zeal and for his Cromwellian enthusiasm rather than for his poetic gifts.

At the turn of the century his reputation as a lyrical poet began to rise, Bowles praising him for his precise delineation of Nature in a passage from 'Upon Appleton House':

> Then as I carless on the Bed
> Of gelid *Straw-berryes* do tread,
> And through the Hazles thick espy
> The hatching *Thrastles* shining Eye ...
>
> (529–32)

As the nineteenth century wore on such diverse critics as Campbell, Hazlitt, Lamb, Miss Mitford, Emerson, Poe and FitzGerald recognized the rare quality of Marvell's verse. Palgrave, doubtless prompted by Tennyson, his friend and mentor, paid Marvell the tribute of including three of his poems in *The Golden Treasury*—'An Horatian Ode', 'The Garden' and 'Bermudas'. He did not print 'To His Coy Mistress', confessedly out of deference to the prudery of his age, although Tennyson, with his characteristic admiration for vigorous magnificence,[1] regarded it as a sublime poem. The Victorians

[1] Tennyson also spoke in the highest terms of Rochester's 'A Satyr Against Mankind'.

admired Marvell as a lyrical poet who celebrated Nature with a remarkable purity and insight, whereas for the past fifty years the revival of interest in the seventeenth-century Metaphysicals has directed our attention to qualities in Marvell's verse which our grandfathers ignored or undervalued, above all to the irony and wit that lie coiled beneath the surface of his poetry. Indeed, some of the recent scholarship and critical ingenuity lavished upon his poems appears to be misplaced; for, while it is undeniable that he was a highly subtle writer, certain critics have attributed to him philosophical implications and verbal ambiguities of which he himself was unaware. Marvell's poetry displays and fuses into a harmonious whole a rich Metaphysical subtlety, a moral seriousness and a sensuous lyricism, part of its fascination residing in the ordered interplay of these varied elements. Before passing on to examine individual poems, we must first consider the operation and the relative importance of these elements in his verse.

Metaphysical poetry habitually displays certain qualities which, though closely interrelated, are yet distinct from one another. It is primarily concerned with problems deriving from or akin to the ancient problem of the One and the Many, body and soul, mind and body, transience and permanence, mortality and immortality, unity-in-duality. Because it is preoccupied with such teasing perplexities, it will tend either to reveal a sense of strain or, at the best, to attain only a momentary poise after which the mind will again pursue the ramifications and apparent contradictions of truth. There must be in a good Metaphysical poem a ceaseless tension and also an intellectual control, which can be achieved only by a use of the Metaphysical conceit. The conceit is not designed to be a fanciful hyperbole, an extravagant adornment or an exuberant manifestation of Baroque energy, although it may sink into being no more than these things. Its true purpose is to fuse the warring elements of the poem into a unity which will intensify the vitality of each element and yet enable them to cohere.

Marvell's poetry fully answers to this description of Metaphysical poetry. The mere titles of some poems—'A Dialogue between the Soul and Body', 'A Dialogue Between The

Resolved Soul, and Created Pleasure'—hint at his obsession with the central problem that Metaphysical poetry attempts to solve. In the Garden poems the various light of the created world is contrasted with the unchanging radiance of eternity, and the two great love poems, 'The Definition of Love' and 'To His Coy Mistress', convey with a vibrant intensity the poet's awareness of paradox and of man's perpetually thwarted desire to transcend his ordained limitations.

The poise and balance which Metaphysical poetry demands are everywhere visible in Marvell's verse, even in the slightest of his poems such as 'Mourning' or 'The Mower to the Glo-Worms', and notably in his finest and most ambitious poems such as 'An Horatian Ode', where the divergent elements are kept under perfect control.

Moreover, one can find in Marvell every type of Metaphysical conceit, ranging from the ingenious pun to the highly serious and even tragic conceit that resolves all contradictions in a flash. Pierre Legouis has remarked that Marvell was indebted in his satirical poems to Cleveland, a notorious exponent of the witty conceit, and in his amorous poems to John Donne. In Part II of *The Rehearsal Transpros'd* (1673), he quotes from Donne's 'The Progress of the Soul' a singularly inapposite passage coupling Luther with Mahomet, as if he wishes to pay tribute to a writer whom he had loved in his youth, and who had long been out of fashion.

It must be confessed that many of Marvell's conceits, however charming, are fanciful and even at times a shade ludicrous, though one suspects that Marvell cherished an affection for some of his more outrageous inventions. The most famous example of a deliberate indulgence in Clevelandism occurs in the last stanza of 'Upon Appleton House':

> But now the *Salmon-Fishers moist*,
> Their *Leathern Boats* begin to hoist;
> And, like *Antipodes* in Shoes,
> Have shod their *Heads* in their *Canoos*.
> How *Tortoise like*, but not so slow,
> These rational *Amphibii* go?   (769–74)

Yet the best of Marvell's conceits are free of such flaws, and

15

reveal the fineness of his perceptions no less than the elegance of his wit:

> What in the World most fair appears,
> Yea even Laughter, turns to Tears:
> And all the Jewels which we prize,
> Melt in these Pendants of the Eyes.
>
> 'Eyes and Tears'

> And, while vain Pomp does her restrain
> Within her solitary Bowr,
> She courts her self in am'rous Rain;
> Her self both *Danae* and the Showr.
>
> 'Mourning'

> Gentler times for Love are ment.
> Who for parting pleasure strain
> Gather Roses in the rain,
> Wet themselves and spoil their Sent.
>
> 'Daphnis and Chloe'

It is a proof of Marvell's candour and suppleness of mind that when drawing upon his recollection of solemn Biblical passages he should have still employed the same witty tone, even where to us it may appear incongruous, as in 'Daphnis and Chloe' where, immediately after a reference to the ravishment of a warm corpse, there occurs a Biblical allusion to the death that overtook the Jews in the wilderness while the manna and quails remained unchewed in their mouths. Happier examples may be found in 'Upon Appleton House', stanza XLVII, where Marvell recalls a passage from Numbers 13:33 about the sons of Anak and, two stanzas later, refers to the crossing of the Red Sea by the Israelites:

> And now to the Abbyss I pass
> Of that unfathomable Grass,
> Where Men like Grashoppers appear,
> But Grashoppers are Gyants there:
> They, in there squeking Laugh, contemn
> Us as we walk more low then them:
> And, from the Precipices tall
> Of the green spir's, to us do call....

The tawny Mowers enter next;
Who seem like *Israalites* to be,
Walking on foot through a green Sea.
To them the Grassy Deeps divide,
And crowd a Lane to either side.

Marvell also employs with supreme art the serious and tragic pun. His grief at the ravages of the Civil Wars was deep and lasting, yet in 'Upon Appleton House' he chooses to express this sense of loss by an almost light-hearted word-play:

Unhappy! shall we never more
That sweet *Militia* restore,
When Gardens only had their Towrs,
And all the Garrisons were Flowrs,
When Roses only Arms might bear,
And Men did rosie Garlands wear?
Tulips, in several Colours barr'd,
Were then the *Switzers* of our *Guard*.   (329–36)

In the description of Charles I on the scaffold in 'An Horatian Ode':

But with his keener Eye
The Axes edge did try   (59–60)

the Latin word *acies* means both eyesight and blade, and, in neo-Platonism, denotes the intent inward gaze of the mind. The lines that depict Cromwell living, in his early days, reserved and austere,

As if his highest plot
To plant the Bergamot   (31–2)

probably contain not only a pun on the word plot, but a suggestion that faint inklings of a royal destiny may even then have flickered through Cromwell's mind, for the bergamot was known as 'the pear of Kings'. As a last example of this device we may take the passage from 'The First Anniversary' in which Cromwell is compared with Amphion, who raised cities by the power of his lute:

Such was that wondrous Order and Consent,
When *Cromwell* tun'd the ruling Instrument.

(67–8)

The Platonic musical symbolism is grounded in the historical fact that in 1653 the Instrument of Government established Cromwell's Protectorate.

That moral seriousness which is the second noteworthy element in Marvell's poetry pervades almost everything that he wrote. We can discern it most clearly in the poems where he overtly rejects the pleasures of the senses and even of the arts, but it informs so apparently slight a poem as 'Clorinda and Damon' in which Damon thrusts aside the temptations proffered by Clorinda:

> C. Near this, a Fountaines liquid Bell
> Tinkles within the concave Shell.
> D. Might a Soul bath there and be clean,
> Or slake its Drought?

Moreover, his concern for social order, his feeling for the unspoiled life of the countryside, and his admiration for the values fostered by great country houses rooted in local tradition give his poetry a fine, mature dignity. A humble gratitude for God's bounty informs his sense of Nature as a divine theatre alive with symbols and hieroglyphs, a sense which is implicit in the Garden poems and explicit in 'Bermudas' where, after enumerating the luxuriant fruits and trees, Marvell proclaims the true glory of the islands:

> He cast (of which we rather boast)
> The Gospels Pearl upon our Coast.
> And in these Rocks for us did frame
> A Temple, where to sound his Name.
> Oh let our Voice his Praise exalt,
> Till it arrive at Heavens Vault:
> Which thence (perhaps) rebounding, may
> Eccho beyond the *Mexique Bay*.
> Thus sung they, in the *English* boat,
> An holy and a chearful Note,
> And all the way to guide their Chime,
> With falling Oars they kept the time.   (29–40)

Those adjectives 'holy' and 'chearful' suggest the distinctive blend and quality of Marvell's Puritanism.

His inner harmony and balance are reflected in the tone of his voice. Like Ben Jonson, whose influence, coupled with that of Spenser, came if not to supplant at least to temper the extravagance of his early Clevelandism, Marvell speaks with the unaffected ease of a man sure of his place in society talking to his equals. We find in him a courtly elegance, a poised, alert wit, an urbane irony that never degenerates into cheap cynicism, a fierce passion far removed from the licentious insolence of the Restoration song-writers, and an assured sense of values which frees him to relish the small joys of life without guilt because he has made his peace with things of great account.

Finally, we must consider the element of lyrical delight, but for which metaphysical wit becomes frigid, and moral strength mere wooden didacticism. The Victorians prized Marvell for the freshness and the intensity of his lyricism, Palgrave comparing him with Shelley and holding 'The Garden' to be 'a test of any reader's insight into the most poetical aspects of poetry'. Modern critics have become shy of praising a poet for his music, though they pride themselves on analysing his tonal modality, and it is more rewarding to demonstrate than to define the exquisite cadences and sensuous delicacy that we find in Marvell's poetry:

> He hangs in shades the Orange bright,
> Like golden Lamps in a green Night.
> And does in the Pomgranates close,
> Jewels more rich than *Ormus* show's.
> He makes the Figs our mouths to meet;
> And throws the Melons at our feet.
>
> 'Bermudas'

> See how it weeps. The Tears do come
> Sad, slowly dropping like a Gumme.
> So weeps the wounded Balsome: so
> The holy Frankincense doth flow.
> The brotherless *Heliades*
> Melt in such Amber Tears as these.
>
> 'The Nymph complaining....'

19

How wide they dream! The *Indian* Slaves
That sink for Pearl through Seas profound,
Would find her Tears yet deeper Waves
And not of one the bottom sound.

'Mourning'

When we have run our Passions heat,
Love hither makes his best retreat.
The *Gods*, that mortal Beauty chase,
Still in a Tree did end their race.
Apollo hunted *Daphne* so,
Only that She might Laurel grow.
And *Pan* did after *Syrinx* speed,
Not as a Nymph, but for a Reed.

'The Garden'

Where you may lye as chast in Bed,
As Pearls together billeted.
All Night embracing Arm in Arm,
Like Chrystal pure with Cotton warm.

'Upon Appleton House'

Unlike two other great Metaphysical poets, Donne and George Herbert, Marvell was not a resourceful inventor of stanzaic forms. In certainty of touch, felicitous graduation of tone, sensitivity of texture and melodic smoothness he is at least their equal; and it was doubtless of these gifts that George Saintsbury was thinking when he said, with pardonable exaggeration, that in 'fingering', the power 'of getting the utmost possible out of metres borrowed or invented—not the greatest poet in English or in literature is Marvell's superior'.

V

We cannot date more than a handful of Marvell's poems with any precision, and since even the most learned critics disagree about their order of composition it may be more helpful to group them roughly according to theme and tone, even if in doing so we are obliged to make certain assumptions about their chronological order. Bearing in mind our ignorance of dates, we may suggest the following crude and tentative grouping:

(i) Verse tributes to Villiers, Hastings and Lovelace; elegant and witty poems on love and on women, such as 'Mourning', 'Eyes and Tears', 'The Match', 'The Fair Singer', 'Daphnis and Chloe', 'The Gallery', 'The Unfortunate Lover'; love poems in the pastoral convention, such as 'Ametas and Thestylis making Hay-Ropes', 'Clorinda and Damon', 'A Dialogue between Thyrsis and Dorinda'. 'Fleckno, an English Priest at Rome' is probably an early poem, since the incidents related in it belong to 1645 or 1646.

(ii) Poems of retreat, contemplation and solitude, including those in which appear the Mower and Juliana; the finest poems in this group are 'The Garden' and 'Upon Appleton House'.

(iii) Poems of Marvell's full maturity on themes of love and death. 'To His Coy Mistress' and 'The Definition of Love' are the outstanding poems in this group, to which we may add 'The Picture of Little T.C. in a Prospect of Flowers' and possibly 'The Nymph complaining for the death of her Faun'.

(iv) Philosophical and religious poems, strongly tinged with a Puritan renunciation of worldly vanity. The outstanding poems in this group are 'On a Drop of Dew', 'A Dialogue Between the Resolved Soul, and Created Pleasure', 'A Dialogue between the Soul and Body', and 'The Coronet'.

(v) Poems celebrating Oliver Cromwell and the Protectorate, notably 'An Horatian Ode', 'The First Anniversary of the Government under O.C.', 'A Poem upon the Death of O.C.'. 'The Character of Holland', 'On the Victory obtained by Blake' and 'Bermudas'.

(vi) Satires of the reign of Charles II.

VI

The early poems of Marvell are occasionally spoiled by a conscious self-indulgence in witty but frigid conceits, yet even in these slight, elegant lyrics one notices the assurance of the poet's control and the delicacy of his touch. In 'Mourning', for example, the poem moves through a succession of faintly cynical reflections upon Chlora's tears, rises to the beautiful penultimate stanza about the Indian slaves diving for pearls and ends with a gravely ironical judgement by the poet:

> I yet my silent Judgment keep,
> Disputing not what they believe:
> But sure as oft as Women weep,
> It is to be suppos'd they grieve.   (33–6)

The gradation of tone is managed with even more subtlety in 'Daphnis and Chloe', where the lover resists the importunities of his mistress who, too late, is bent upon giving herself to him at the very moment of parting. He breaks away from her in anguish, and then suddenly Marvell reverts to a cool speculation about masculine inconstancy and feminine coyness in the game of love:

> At these words away he broke;
> As who long has praying ly'n,
> To his Heads-man makes the Sign,
> And receives the parting stroke.
>
> But hence Virgins all beware.
> Last night he with *Phlogis* slept;
> This night for *Dorinda* kept;
> And but rid to take the Air.
>
> Yet he does himself excuse;
> Nor indeed without a Cause.
> For, according to the Lawes,
> Why did *Chloe* once refuse?   (97–108)

The pastoral poems also occasionally take an unexpected twist, for though Ametas and Thestylis end their duel of wits in the traditional country manner:

> Then let's both lay by our Rope,
> And go kiss within the Hay   (15–16)

Clorinda and Damon turn from love to sing the praise of Pan, and Thyrsis and Dorinda prepare wine steeped in poppies that they may more speedily find Elizium.

VII

Marvell's retreat into the solitude of Appleton House seems to have inspired poetry of a deeper, more reflective nature than any he had composed hitherto. The poems in which the Mower and Juliana appear, though they are partly love poems, and partly poems about the countryside, contain some darker and more serious undertones. Death is present and with his scythe mimics the destruction wrought upon the grass by the mower and upon the mower by Juliana:

> For *Juliana* comes, and She
> What I do to the Grass, does to my Thoughts and Me.

Marvell reflects also upon man's relationship with Nature, and upon the way in which his ordering of the countryside is both a perfecting and yet a perversion of Nature:

> His green *Seraglio* has its Eunuchs too;
>   Lest any Tyrant him out-doe.
> And in the Cherry he does Nature vex,
>   To procreate without a Sex.[1]

The world of Nature held for Marvell a profound moral and spiritual import. Unlike Randolph and the French libertine poets, who used the garden as a symbol to inculcate a naturalist glorification of sensual indulgence, Marvell depicts it as the *hortus conclusus*, the enclosed garden of *The Song of Songs*, where the withdrawn and solitary intellect may pass beyond the senses and contemplate the Divine. We need not pause to investigate the precise debt (if any) that Marvell owed to Bonaventura, Hugh of St Victor, Richard of St Victor, Plotinus, Ficino, Hermes Trismegistus, Lipsius, the Divine Casimire, or any other candidates advanced by ingenious commentators and source-hunters. Such refinements of scholarship may serve to strengthen our understanding of 'The Garden' and 'Upon Appleton House'; but our first task must be to respond, by an exercise of imaginative sympathy, to the images and symbols which he employs in these poems of contemplative ecstasy.

'Upon Appleton House', for all its brilliance and variety, has seemed to many readers a muddled and uneven poem, because in it Marvell is trying to counterpoint a number of complex and diverse themes. He desires to pay a courtly, reasoned compliment to the Fairfaxes, and in the process to convey his admiration of the secure, harmonious life which a country house guarantees. This leads him to survey the

[1] The reference is probably to the stoneless cherry.

history of the house, in the course of which he attacks the Catholic technique of sensual sublimation, contrasting it with the Puritan ideal personified in Mary Fairfax, a child soon to become a woman. Fairfax's retirement from politics is lamented, because he might have saved England from the desolation which threatens it, the notion of England as a garden inspiring Marvell to a characteristically poignant, yet witty, stanza:

> Oh Thou, that dear and happy Isle
> The Garden of the World ere while,
> Thou *Paradise* of four Seas,
> Which *Heaven* planted us to please,
> But, to exclude the World, did guard
> With watry if not flaming Sword;
> What luckless Apple did we tast,
> To make us Mortal, and The Wast?   (321–8)

Marvell then passes to the central portion of the poem, his retreat into the countryside surrounding the house. The precise and loving description of the creatures thronging the woods, meadows and pools; an evocation of nature's teeming, elaborate richness; the play of a shimmering wit upon the objects of the poet's contemplation; a quaint humour, a steady piety and a soaring ecstasy are entwined by Marvell in this poem with consummate artifice. He draws from the sight of the birds, insects, trees and plants the certainty reserved for those who find a pattern behind the fluctuations of the visible world, and rejoices in the strength that comes from rural solitude:

> Already I begin to call
> In their most learned Original:
> And where I Language want, my Signs
> The Bird upon the Bough divines;
> And more attentive there doth sit
> Then if She were with Lime-twigs knit.
> No Leaf does tremble in the Wind
> Which I returning cannot find.

Out of these scatter'd *Sibyls* Leaves
Strange *Prophecies* my Phancy weaves:
And in one History consumes,
Like *Mexique Paintings*, all the *Plumes*.
What *Rome, Greece, Palestine*, ere said
I in this light *Mosaick* read.
Thrice happy he who, not mistook,
Hath read in *Natures mystick Book*....   (569–84)

How safe, methinks, and strong, behind
These Trees have I incamp'd my Mind;
Where Beauty, aiming at the Heart,
Bends in some Tree its useless Dart;
And where the World no certain Shot
Can make, or me it toucheth not.
But I on it securely play,
And gaul its Horsemen all the Day.   (601–8)

There follow stanzas that combine a formal compliment to
Mary Fairfax with a description of nightfall:

The modest *Halcyon* comes in sight
Flying betwixt the Day and Night;
And such an horror calm and dumb,
Admiring Nature does benum.

The viscous Air, wheres' ere She fly,
Follows and sucks her Azure dy;
The gellying Stream compacts below,
If it might fix her shadow so;
The stupid Fishes hang, as plain
As *Flies* in *Chrystal* overt'ane;
And Men the silent *Scene* assist,
Charm'd with the *Saphir-winged Mist*.

Maria such, and so doth hush
The World, and through the *Ev'ning* rush
                (669–82)

After the praise of Mary Fairfax is concluded, this brilliant
poem draws to its close with the conceit about the salmon-
fishers, and with a final couplet that reinforces our sense of
having traversed a world of rich sensual experience, now subject to the dark:

> Let's in: for the dark *Hemisphere*
> Does now like one of them appear.   (775–6)

'The Garden', though it is shorter and less widely-ranging than 'Upon Appleton House', is at once the most sensuous and the most philosophical of all Marvell's poems. Its concealed puns, tantalizing ambiguities and metaphysical complexity have, in recent years, given rise to many learned commentaries. Scholars have minutely investigated the sources and the precise connotation of the images which Marvell employs with such certainty and lyrical resonance—the bird waving its plumes, the melon, the garden itself; while the single word 'green' (a favourite word of Marvell's) has been interpreted by reference to Renaissance colour-symbolism, hermetic speculation and medieval neo-Platonism, though in this context it is almost certainly meant to conjure up associations of freshness and innocence. Yet for all the latent word-play and subtle undertones which mould and colour the poem, its central theme is clearly defined.

After deprecating human ambition, Marvell launches into the praise of woodland solitude, contrasting the green of plants and trees with the emblematic colours of female beauty, white and red:

> No white nor red was ever seen
> So am'rous as this lovely green.   (17–18)

Even the god's pursuit of Daphne and Syrinx has as its true end their metamorphosis into laurel and reed.

Then follow three stanzas, which bring together the poem's leading motifs:

> What wond'rous Life in this I lead!
> Ripe Apples drop about my head;
> The Luscious Clusters of the Vine
> Upon my Mouth do crush their Wine;
> The Nectaren, and curious Peach,
> Into my hands themselves do reach;
> Stumbling on Melons, as I pass,
> Insnar'd with Flow'rs, I fall on Grass.
>
> Mean while the Mind, from pleasure less,
> Withdraws into its happiness;

The Mind, that Ocean where each kind
Does streight its own resemblance find;
Yet it creates, transcending these,
Far other Worlds, and other Seas;
Annihilating all that's made
To a green Thought in a green Shade.[1]

Here at the Fountains sliding foot,
Or at some Fruit-trees mossy-root,
Casting the Bodies Vest aside,
My Soul into the boughs does glide:
There like a Bird it sits, and sings,
Then whets, and combs its silver Wings;
And, till prepar'd for longer flight,
Waves in its Plumes the various Light.   (33–48)

In this paradisal Garden, Woman being absent, even the Fall
is innocent, as the contemplative soul prepares for its flight
towards God.

Finally, after the rapt vision of these stanzas, Marvell returns
again to the garden where Woman is excluded but where the
industrious bee, symbol of social order, computes Time,
which is itself dependent on the living flowers woven into
that sophisticated invention of man, the floral sundial:

How well the skilful Gardner drew
Of flow'rs and herbes this Dial new;
Where from above the milder Sun
Does through a fragrant Zodiack run;
And, as it works, th' industrious Bee
Computes its time as well as we.
How could such sweet and wholsome Hours
Be reckon'd but with herbs and flow'rs!   (65–72)

Less brilliant and ingenious than 'Upon Appleton House',
'The Garden' has a sustained piety and gravity, a perfectly
controlled sensuous melody and a profound yet delicate wit
that Marvell never surpassed. If indeed 'The Garden' was
composed at Appleton House and was the last poem he wrote
before quitting the Fairfax household for the 'uncessant
labours' of public life, it was a worthy farewell.

[1] Margoliouth's note brings out the ambiguity of this couplet: 'either
"reducing the whole material world to nothing material, i.e. to a green
thought", or "considering the whole material world as of no value compared to a green thought".'

VIII

Although Marvell insisted that there was no place for Woman in the Garden, he wrote two love poems of the highest quality, one of which celebrates with passionate conviction the power and ardour of physical desire. Yet even in 'To His Coy Mistress', Marvell's customary wit and intellectual control do not desert him, the poem unfolding with the rigorous exactitude of a medieval syllogism. It opens with a quiet, conversational remark:

> Had we but World enough, and Time,
> This coyness Lady were no crime.

In a series of extravagant conceits the lover assures his mistress that he would prolong his love-making indefinitely,

> And you should if you please refuse
> Till the Conversion of the *Jews*　　(9–10)

which, according to ancient tradition, would take place immediately before the end of the world. Then follows the second movement of the poem which, though logically inevitable, achieves a poetic surprise by its swift change of tone:

> But at my back I alwaies hear
> Times winged Charriot hurrying near:
> And yonder all before us lye
> Desarts of vast Eternity.
> Thy Beauty shall no more be found;
> Nor, in thy marble Vault, shall sound
> My ecchoing Song: then Worms shall try
> That long preserv'd Virginity:
> And your quaint Honour turn to dust;
> And into ashes all my Lust.
> The Grave's a fine and private place,
> But none I think do there embrace.　　(21–32)

Finally, the lover demands that he and his mistress should enjoy what John Donne calls 'the right true end of love'; yet despite the uncompromising sexuality of the lines quoted above and of the imagery in the poem's concluding lines, Marvell has invested the old classical commonplace of *carpe diem* with an intensity and a nobility that seem to affirm the triumph of love over time, in the teeth of the evidence:

> Let us roll all our Strength, and all
> Our sweetness, up into one Ball:
> And tear our Pleasures with rough strife,
> Thorough the Iron gates of Life.
> Thus, though we cannot make our Sun
> Stand still, yet we will make him run.   (41–6)

'The Definition of Love', though far less sensuous than 'To His Coy Mistress', conveys with equal force the longing of two lovers to be united:

> And yet I quickly might arrive
> Where my extended Soul is fixt,
> But Fate does Iron wedges drive,
> And alwaies crouds it self betwixt.   (9–12)

By means of geometrical and astronomical images Marvell develops the paradox that the lovers' separation is a proof of their spiritual correspondence, and a guarantee of their spiritual union:

> As Lines so Loves *oblique* may well
> Themselves in every Angle greet:
> But ours so truly *Paralel*,
> Though infinite can never meet.
>
> Therefore the Love which us doth bind,
> But Fate so enviously debarrs,
> Is the Conjunction of the Mind,
> And Opposition of the Stars.   (25–32)

'The Picture of little T.C. in a Prospect of Flowers', differing as it does in theme and tone from the love poems, reminds us that fate and death shatter the most innocent dreams of youthful love. Little T.C., 'this Darling of the Gods', plays among the flowers, courted by Nature, aware only of life. In the third stanza Marvell introduces the image of the shade:

> Let me be laid,
> Where I may see thy Glories from some shade
> (23–4)

29

as though to prepare for the sudden turn of the poem in the final stanza, where the shadow of death falls upon this Arcady:

> But O young beauty of the Woods,
> Whom Nature courts with fruits and flow'rs,
> Gather the Flow'rs, but spare the Buds;
> Lest *Flora* angry at thy crime,
> To kill her Infants in their prime,
> Do quickly make th' Example Yours;
>   And, ere we see,
> Nip in the blossome all our hopes and Thee.[1]
>
>   (33–40)

There is still much controversy about the significance of 'The Nymph complaining for the death of her Faun'. To regard it as the lament of an Anglican for his stricken Church, or as a conscious allegory of the Church's love for Christ crucified, borders on the improbable: this is not to deny that there are in it unmistakable references to *The Song of Songs* or that Marvell allowed these symbolic overtones to deepen the poem's imaginative richness and to enlarge its range. Overtly and primarily, it remains the lament of a young girl for her fawn, given to her by a faithless lover. The rhythm, the diction and the imagery are so dramatically appropriate that many readers will be content to accept the poem at its face value or, if they feel compelled to probe for a hidden meaning, may find in it a lamentation for love destroyed, not by time, fate or death, but by the sinful inconstancy of man.

IX

Marvell, though a sensual and a religious man, did not, like Crashaw, explore the relation between divine and erotic love, for such a procedure would have been repugnant to his fastidious temperament even if it had not run counter to his doctrinal beliefs. He was indeed acutely aware of the conflicts between the warring impulses within himself, two of his dialogues being variations on this theme. In one of them, 'A Dialogue Between the Resolved Soul, and Created Pleasure', the

---

[1] If T.C. is Theophila Cornewall, these lines take on an added poignancy for she was named after an elder sister who died in infancy.

soul wins the battle a shade too easily, the Chorus celebrating
the victory with an operatic flourish:

> Triumph, triumph, victorious Soul;
> The World has not one Pleasure more:
> The rest does lie beyond the Pole,
> And is thine everlasting Store.

The scales are poised more evenly in 'A Dialogue between
the Soul and Body', which opens with the complaint of the
soul:

> O who shall, from this Dungeon, raise
> A Soul inslav'd so many wayes?
> With bolts of Bones, that fetter'd stands
> In Feet; and manacled in Hands.
> Here blinded with an Eye; and there
> Deaf with the drumming of an Ear.   (1–6)

Yet the body, which rebels against the even more insidious
tyranny of the soul, is granted the last word:

> What but a Soul could have the wit
> To build me up for Sin so fit?
> So Architects do square and hew,
> Green Trees that in the Forest grew.   (41–4)

One commentator on this poem has challenged the con-
ventional view that it is deeply rooted in Christian theology,
accusing Marvell of displaying a callous, vicious cynicism and
a 'deliberate indifferentism' to the problems of existence.[1]
There can be no disputing the fact that in the most moving
of all his religious poems Marvell unequivocally renounces
the subtlest lures of the world, sacrificing even the long-
cherished illusion that his poems are garlands woven for
Christ's head, and acknowledging that the Serpent lies hidden
there. 'The Coronet' invites comparison with George Herbert's 'The Collar' in the exactitude with which its fluctuating
rhythm mirrors the twists and turns of the recalcitrant spirit,
in the harmonious progression of its imagery, and in the

[1] A. Birrell in *The Downside Review*, No. 232, 1955.

unaffected humility and grace of the poet's final surrender
to God:

> But thou who only could'st the Serpent tame,
> Either his slipp'ry Knots at once untie,
> And disintangle all his winding Snare:
> Or shatter too with him my curious frame:
> And let these wither, so that he may die,
> Though set with Skill, and chosen out with Care.
> That they, while Thou on both their Spoils dost tread,
> May crown thy Feet, that could not crown thy Head.
>
> (19–26)

X

'An Horatian Ode upon Cromwel's Return from Ireland',
presumably written in the early summer of 1650, was one
of the three Cromwell poems which have been cancelled by
the printer in all but two surviving copies of the 1681 *Miscellaneous Poems*. This alone casts grave doubts upon the modern
supposition that it is a Royalist poem, though the mere fact
that reputable scholars can put forward this hypothesis is a
tribute to the extraordinary balance which Marvell preserved
in the greatest of his political verses.

In 1672 Marvell wrote of the Civil Wars:

> I think the cause was too good to have been fought for.... For
> men may spare their pains where nature is at work, and the world
> will not go the faster for our driving. Even as his present Majestie's
> happy Restoration did it self, so all things else happen in their best
> and proper time, without any need of our officiousness.

A similar recognition of historical necessity informs the
'Ode', enabling Marvell to pay tribute to Charles I's serene
courage upon the scaffold, and yet to acknowledge that his
blood had to flow before new order could be created out of
chaotic violence:

> *He* nothing common did or mean
> Upon that memorable Scene:
> But with his keener Eye
> The Axes edge did try:

Nor call'd the *Gods* with vulgar spight
To vindicate his helpless Right,
    But bow'd his comely Head,
    Down as upon a Bed.
This was that memorable Hour
Which first assur'd the forced Pow'r.
    So when they did design
    The *Capitols* first Line,
A bleeding Head where they begun,
Did fright the Architects to run;
    And yet in that the *State*
    Foresaw it's happy Fate.   (57–72)

Marvell speaks of Cromwell with a kind of horrified awe, as if he were a destructive aspect of Nature, like three-forked lightning:

    Then burning through the Air he went,
    And Pallaces and Temples rent.   (21–2)

So, in Marvell's eyes, all the ruthless, destructive acts of Cromwell—the trapping of Charles at Carisbrooke, the massacre of the Irish, the coming subjugation of the Scots— are justified, because he is the product of fate:

    But thou the Wars and Fortunes Son
    March indefatigably on;   (113–14)

and because, like a falcon, he still remains obedient to England, the falconer.

The puns, ironies and ambiguities which give this 'Ode' its peculiar tension cease to be puzzling once we understand how deeply all are imbued with Marvell's exultant sense of religious destiny that finds so perfect an expression in the weighty grandeur of the poem's metre and language.

Of the remaining poems written during the Common- wealth only 'Bermudas' recaptures the impassioned vision of a divinely ordered society living in harmony with itself.[1] The other two Cromwell poems, for all their energy and formal splendour, reveal a sense of strain, even of desperation, as if

---

[1] It had, however, taken a Cromwellian fleet in 1651 to convert the colony to the Puritan cause.

Marvell were aware that between England and chaos there stood only Cromwell, depicted as a cross between a Hebrew warrior-statesman and a neo-Platonic mythological hero. By 1658 Marvell is moving away from the beautifully poised assurance of the earlier poems to the reiterated bludgeoning violence of the post-Restoration satires.

XI

Scholars still disagree about which of the satires attributed to Marvell are in fact by him, and it is unwise to be dogmatic about their authorship. Opinions also differ about the merits of those satires that are probably authentic: it is possible to argue that they do not represent a sad decline in Marvell's genius; but once we have allowed that they possess the rollicking vigour of good street ballads and a certain rough effectiveness we have said almost all there is to be said in their favour. The lines on young Douglas's death, and the setpiece on the vision of England which appears to Charles II (both in 'The Last Instructions to a Painter') glow with something of Marvell's former ardour:

> Like a glad Lover, the fierce Flames he meets,
> And tries his first embraces in their Sheets.
> His shape exact, which the bright flames infold,
> Like the Sun's Statue stands of burnish'd Gold.
> Round the transparent Fire about him glows,
> As the clear Amber on the Bee does close:
> And, as on Angels Heads their Glories shine,
> His burning Locks adorn his Face Divine...
>
> (677–84)

> Paint last the King, and a dead shade of Night,
> Only dispers'd by a weak Tapers light;
> And those bright gleams that dart along and glare
> From his clear Eyes, yet these too dark with Care.
> There, as in the calm horrour all alone,
> He wakes and Muses of th' uneasie Throne:
> Raise up a sudden Shape with Virgins Face,
> Though ill agree her Posture, Hour, or Place:
> Naked as born, and her round Arms behind,
> With her own Tresses interwove and twin'd:

34

Her mouth lock't up, a blind before her Eyes,
Yet from beneath the Veil her blushes rise;
And silent tears her secret anguish speak,
Her heart throbs, and with very shame would break.

(885–98)

More typical of the satires are the following passages, one taken from 'The Statue in Stocks-Market', describing Sir Robert Viner's statue of Charles II, and one from 'A Dialogue between the Two Horses':

But Sir Robert affirms we do him much wrong;
For the graver's at work to reform him thus long.
But alas! he will never arrive at his end,
For 'tis such a king as no chisel can mend.... (53–6)

More Tolerable are the Lion Kings Slaughters
Than the Goats making whores of our wives and our daughters.
The Debauch'd and the Bloody since they Equally Gall us,
I had rather Bare Nero than Sardanapalus, (131–4)

The satires are, like *The Rehearsal Transpros'd*, larded with crude jokes about vomiting, the bodily functions and venereal disease; and spiced with wild accusations of secret crimes and unnatural vice. Unlike Dryden and Pope, who are equally obscene but who contrive by sheer energy and artifice to transcend their dirtiness, Marvell all too frequently gets stuck in his own filth. The fact seems to be that as he grew older Marvell, for reasons which we can only conjecture, suffered an emotional or even a physiological coarsening which betrays itself in the very rhythms of his later poetry.

Yet Marvell himself might have believed the price worth paying in order to safeguard the liberties of England. All the poems published in his lifetime sprang from a desire to celebrate a public occasion, pay tribute to a friend, or attack a specific evil, the later satires conforming precisely to Marvell's conception of the poet's task as defined in 'Tom May's Death':

When the Sword glitters ore the Judges head,
And fear has Coward Churchmen silenced,

Then is the Poets time, 'tis then he drawes,
And single fights forsaken Vertues cause.
He, when the wheel of Empire, whirleth back,
And though the World's disjointed Axel crack,
Sings still of ancient Rights and better Times,
Seeks wretched good, arraigns successful Crimes.

(63–70)

Marvell's lonely and perilous opposition to Charles II's government matches in faith and courage the defiant gesture of the Cavalier Sir Robert Shirley, whose epitaph in Staunton Harold church records that

in the year 1653, when all things sacred were throughout the nation either demollisht or profaned, Sir Robert Shirley baronet founded this church, whose singular praise it is to have done the best things in the worst times, and hoped them in the most calamituous.

Even if it is true that Marvell's place in English literature is secure only because he wrote a handful of lyrics which display an intuitive moral and aesthetic certainty as rare as the perfection of their phrasing, to concentrate on them alone would be to distort Marvell's true image. The dusty political and religious causes for which he laboured in the last twenty years of his life, although to us they may seem not worth the devotion he gave them, were to Marvell of supreme importance. Had he cared less passionately for things other than poetry his verse might have lacked the urgency, the gravity and the resolute dignity that lend it so fine a distinction. Little as we may concern ourselves with the quarrels of seventeenth-century Englishmen, and with the part which Marvell played in them, we shall find that a lively sympathy for the aspirations of the puritan and the patriot will help us to understand more fully the achievement and the stature of the poet.

36

ANDREW MARVELL

A Select Bibliography

(Place of publication London, unless stated otherwise)

Bibliography:

ANDRÉ MARVELL: Poète, Puritain, Patriote, 1621–1678, par P. Legouis; Paris and London (1928)

—contains a full, annotated bibliography, including a list of prose works attributed to Marvell.

ANDREW MARVELL, 1927–1967, by D. G. Donovan (1969)

—one of the 'Elizabethan Bibliographies Supplements'.

A CONCORDANCE TO THE ENGLISH POEMS OF ANDREW MARVELL, by G. R. Guffey; Chapel Hill (1974).

Collected and Selected Works:

MISCELLANEOUS POEMS (1681)

—in all but two recorded copies the three Cromwell poems have been cancelled. One of these copies, preserved in the British Museum, contains 'An Horatian Ode', 'The First Anniversary' and 'A Poem upon the Death of O.C.', lines 1–184. A reprint of the British Museum copy was published in a limited edition by the Nonesuch Press in 1923.

THE WORKS, ed. T. Cooke, 2 vols (1726)

—contains the 1681 poems, State Poems, the Greek and the Latin poems in honour of Princess Anne's birth, a short life of Marvell and a few letters. Reissued in 1772.

THE WORKS, ed. E. Thompson, 3 vols (1776)

—contains all the letters and poems of Cooke's edition, some new poems and satires, a life, the bulk of the *Corporation Letters* and a few private letters. A completely uncritical edition, containing poems which are certainly not by Marvell.

THE WORKS, ed. A. B. Grosart, 4 vols; Blackburn (1872–5)

—the first two volumes (I. Poems, II. Letters) have been superseded by Margoliouth, but Vols. III and IV, with all their faults, are the only available collection of Marvell's prose writings. In the Fuller Worthies' Library.

POEMS AND SATIRES, ed. E. Wright (1904).

POEMS AND LETTERS, ed. H. M. Margoliouth, 2 vols; Oxford (1927)

—Vol. I Poems, Vol. II Letters. The definitive edition, in the Oxford English Texts. The third edition, 1971, revised by P.

Legouis, contains eight new letters and the results of recent scholarly research.

SELECTED POETRY AND PROSE, ed. D. Davison (1952)

—contains most of the poetry and a little of the prose. The editor's introduction is well worth studying.

THE POEMS, ed. H. Macdonald (1952)

—a reprint of the unique British Museum copy of the 1681 edition, with some additional poems. In the Muses' Library, superseding the original Muses' Library edition in 2 vols, edited by H. Aitken, 1892.

THE LATIN POETRY OF ANDREW MARVELL, ed. W. A. McQueen and K. A. Rockwell; Chapel Hill (1964).

SELECTED POETRY, ed. F. Kermode; New York (1967).

COMPLETE POETRY, ed. G. de F. Lord; New York (1968).

THE REHEARSAL TRANSPROS'D and THE REHEARSAL TRANSPROS'D, THE SECOND PART, ed. D. I. B. Smith; Oxford (1971).

THE COMPLETE POEMS, ed. E. S. Donno; Harmondsworth (1972).

Separate Works:

AN ELEGY UPON THE DEATH OF MY LORD FRANCIS VILLIERS [1648]. *Verse*

—undated and unique copy is at Worcester College, Oxford. On the reasons for believing it to be by Marvell see Margoliouth, I, pp. 432–6.

THE CHARACTER OF HOLLAND (1665). *Verse*

—appeared anonymously.

THE REHEARSAL TRANSPROS'D... (1672). *Prose*

—appeared anonymously, probably printed in London.

THE REHEARSAL TRANSPROS'D: THE SECOND PART... (1673) *Prose*

MR. SMIRKE: OR, THE DIVINE IN MODE... (1677). *Prose*

—appeared anonymously.

A SHORT HISTORICAL ESSAY... (1677). *Prose*

AN ACCOUNT OF THE GROWTH OF POPERY AND ARBITRARY GOVERNMENT IN ENGLAND...; Amsterdam (1677). *Prose*

—appeared anonymously.

REMARKS UPON A LATE DISINGENUOUS DISCOURSE... (1678). *Prose*

—appeared anonymously.

Some Biographical and Critical Studies:

THE LIFE OF ANDREW MARVELL..., by J. Dove (1832).

ANDREW MARVELL, by A. Birrell (1905)

—in the 'English Men of Letters' series.

ANDRÉ MARVELL: Poète, Puritain, Patriote, 1621–78, par P. Legouis; Paris and London (1928)

—a masterly biographical and critical survey. Abridged English version, 1965. See below.

ANDREW MARVELL, by V. Sackville-West (1929).

THE DONNE TRADITION, by G. Williamson; Oxford (1930).

SEVEN TYPES OF AMBIGUITY, by W. Empson (1930).

SELECTED ESSAYS, by T. S. Eliot (1932)
—contains 'The Metaphysical Poets', first printed in *The Times Literary Supplement*, 20, xi. 1921, pp. 669–70; and 'Andrew Marvell', first printed in *The Times Literary Supplement*, 31, iii, 1921, pp. 201–3; and reprinted in *Andrew Marvell, 1621– 78: Tercentenary Tributes*, 1922.

DETERMINATIONS, ed. F. R. Leavis (1934)
—contains 'Marvell's Garden', by W. Empson and 'On Metaphysical Poetry', by J. Smith.

SOME VERSIONS OF PASTORAL, by W. Empson (1935).

REVALUATION, by F. R. Leavis (1936)
—contains an important essay, 'The Line of Wit'.

FROM DONNE TO DRYDEN: The Revolt against Metaphysical poetry, by R. L. Sharp; Chapel Hill (1940).

ANDREW MARVELL, by M. C. Bradbrook and M. G. Lloyd Thomas; Cambridge (1940).
—a scholarly and original study, packed with stimulating critical observations. An excellent supplement to Legouis. Reprinted with corrections, 1961.

ENGLISH LITERATURE IN THE EARLIER SEVENTEENTH CENTURY, 1600–1660, by D. Bush; Oxford (1945)
—second ed., 1962.

STUDIES IN SEVENTEENTH-CENTURY POETIC, by R. Wallerstein; Madison, Wisconsin (1950)
—a learned and authoritative study of the seventeenth-century philosophical background. The second part of the book is devoted to a discussion of Marvell's poetry, and contains elaborate analyses of individual poems. A difficult book, but a work of great importance.

THE SHAKESPEAREAN MOMENT, by P. Cruttwell (1954).

METAPHYSICAL TO AUGUSTAN by G. Walton; Cambridge (1955)

INTERPRETATIONS, ed. J. Wain (1955)
—contains 'Andrew Marvell: "An Horatian Ode upon Cromwel's Return from Ireland"', by L. D. Lerner.

PURITANISM AND REVOLUTION: Studies in interpretation of the English revolution of the 17th century, by C. Hill (1958)
—contains 'Society and Andrew Marvell', first printed in *Modern Quarterly*, I, iv, 1946.

TRADITION AND POETIC STRUCTURE, by J. V. Cunningham; Denver, Colarado (1960)
—contains a chapter on Marvell.

POETRY AND POLITICS UNDER THE STUARTS, by C. V. Wedgwood; Cambridge (1960).

THE SCHOOL OF DONNE, by A. Alvarez (1961)
—contains a chapter on Marvell.

THE UNTUNING OF THE SKY: Ideas of music in English poetry, 1500–1700, by J. Hollander (1961).

REASON AND THE IMAGINATION, ed. J. A. Mazzeo (1962)
—contains an essay by Mazzeo, 'Cromwell as Davidic king'.

THE HAPPY MAN: Studies in the metamorphosis of a classical ideal, 1600–1700, by M-S. Røstvig; Oslo (1962)
—a revised edition of a work first published in 1954; pp. 152–95 are devoted to Marvell.

POETRY AND THE FOUNTAIN OF LIGHT, by H. R. Swardson (1962)
—contains a chapter on Marvell.

SOME THEMES AND VARIATIONS IN THE POETRY OF ANDREW MARVELL, by J. B. Leishman (1963)
—the British Academy Warton Lecture, 1961.

FIVE METAPHYSICAL POETS, by J. Bennett; Cambridge (1964)
—a revised edition of *Four Metaphysical Poets*, 1934, with an additional chapter on Marvell.

THE POETRY OF ANDREW MARVELL, by D. Davison (1964)
—a brief but admirable discussion of the poetry.

ANDREW MARVELL, by L. W. Hyman; New York (1964).

ANDREW MARVELL: Poet, Puritan, Patriot, 1621–1678, by P. Legouis; Oxford (1965)
—an abridged version in English by Legouis of his great work of 1928. See above. It incorporates and gives references for the large mass of Marvell scholarship produced since the mid–1920s.

NATURAL MAGIC: Studies in the presentation of Nature in English poetry from Spenser to Marvell, by K. M. Scoular; Oxford (1965)
—contains a chapter, 'Upon Appleton House'.

MARVELL'S IRONIC VISION, by H. E. Toliver; New Haven (1965).

THE ART OF MARVELL'S POETRY, by J. B. Leishman (1966)
—second ed., 1968; an erudite study of Marvell's non-satirical poems.

DESTINY HIS CHOICE: The Loyalism of Andrew Marvell, by J. M. Wallace; Cambridge (1968)
—an analysis of Marvell's political attitudes.

ANDREW MARVELL: A Collection of critical essays, ed. G. de F. Lord; Englewood Cliffs (1968).

ANDREW MARVELL: A Critical anthology, ed. J. Carey; Harmondsworth (1969)

—an excellent collection which reprints important articles in full or in part, and extracts from full-length studies. The introductions and other editorial material are admirable.

MARVELL: Modern judgements, ed. M. Wilding (1969)

—a collection of recent critical essays.

THE RESOLVED SOUL: A Study of Marvell's major poems, by A. E. Berthoff; Princeton (1970).

'MY ECCHOING SONG': Andrew Marvell's poetry of criticism, by R. L. Colie; Princeton (1970).

SPENSER, MARVELL, AND RENAISSANCE PASTORAL, by P. Cullen; Cambridge, Mass. (1970).

MARVELL'S PASTORAL ART, by D. M. Friedman (1970).

ENGLISH POETRY AND PROSE, 1540–1674 (1970)

—Vol II of the Sphere *History of Literature in the English Language*, ed. C. Ricks. It contains 'Andrew Marvell and the Caroline Poets', by M-S. Røstvig, pp. 206–48.

MARVELL'S ALLEGORICAL POETRY, by Bruce King; Cambridge (1977).

WRITERS AND THEIR WORK

GRAY: R. W. Ketton Cremer
HUME: Montgomery Belgion
SAMUEL JOHNSON: S. C. Roberts
POPE: Ian Jack
RICHARDSON: R. F. Brissenden
SHERIDAN: W. A. Darlington
SMART: Geoffrey Grigson
SMOLLETT: Laurence Brander
STEELE, ADDISON:
      A. R. Humphreys
STERNE: D. W. Jefferson
SWIFT: J. Middleton Murry (1955)
SWIFT: A. Norman Jeffares (1976)
VANBRUGH: Bernard Harris
HORACE WALPOLE: Hugh Honour

Nineteenth Century:
ARNOLD: Kenneth Allott
AUSTEN:
      S. Townsend Warner (1951)
AUSTEN: B. C. Southam (1975)
BAGEHOT: N. St John-Stevas
THE BRONTË SISTERS:
      Phyllis Bentley (1950)
THE BRONTËS: I & II:
      Winifred Gérin
E. B. BROWNING: Alethea Hayter
ROBERT BROWNING: John Bryson
SAMUEL BUTLER: G. D. H. Cole
BYRON: I, II & III:
      Bernard Blackstone
CARLYLE: David Gascoyne
CARROLL: Derek Hudson
CLOUGH: Isobel Armstrong
COLERIDGE: Kathleen Raine
CREEVEY & GREVILLE:
      J. Richardson
DE QUINCEY: Hugh Sykes Davies
DICKENS: K. J. Fielding
  EARLY NOVELS: Trevor Blount
  LATER NOVELS: Barbara Hardy
DISRAELI: Paul Bloomfield
GEORGE ELIOT: Lettice Cooper
FITZGERALD: Joanna Richardson
GASKELL: Miriam Allott
GISSING: A. C. Ward
HARDY: R. A. Scott-James
      and C. Day Lewis

HAZLITT: J. B. Priestley
HOOD: Laurence Brander
HOPKINS: Geoffrey Grigson
T. H. HUXLEY: William Irvine
KEATS: Edmund Blunden (1950)
KEATS: Miriam Allott (1976)
LAMB: Edmund Blunden
LANDOR: G. Rostrevor Hamilton
LEAR: Joanna Richardson
MACAULAY: G. R. Potter
MACAULAY: Kenneth Young
MEREDITH: Phyllis Bartlett
MILL: Maurice Cranston
MORRIS: Philip Henderson
NEWMAN: J. M. Cameron
PATER: Ian Fletcher
PEACOCK: J. I. M. Stewart
CHRISTINA ROSSETTI:
      G. Battiscombe
D. G. ROSSETTI: Oswald Doughty
RUSKIN: Peter Quennell
SCOTT: Ian Jack
SHELLEY: G. M. Matthews
SOUTHEY: Geoffrey Carnall
STEPHEN: Phyllis Grosskurth
STEVENSON: G. B. Stern
SWINBURNE: Ian Fletcher
TENNYSON: B. C. Southam
THACKERAY: Laurence Brander
FRANCIS THOMPSON: Peter Butter
TROLLOPE: Hugh Sykes Davies
WILDE: James Laver
WORDSWORTH: Helen Darbishire

Twentieth Century:
ACHEBE: A. Ravenscroft
ARDEN: Glenda Leeming
AUDEN: Richard Hoggart
BECKETT: J-J. Mayoux
BENNETT:
      Frank Swinnerton (1950)
BENNETT: Kenneth Young (1975)
BETJEMAN: John Press
BLUNDEN: Alec M. Hardie
BOND: Simon Trussler
BRIDGES: John Sparrow
BURGESS: Carol M. Dix
CAMPBELL: David Wright

CARY: Walter Allen
CHESTERTON: C. Hollis
CHURCHILL: John Connell
COLLINGWOOD: E. W. F. Tomlin
COMPTON-BURNETT:
R. Glynn Grylls
CONRAD: Oliver Warner
DE LA MARE: Kenneth Hopkins
NORMAN DOUGLAS: Ian Greenlees
LAWRENCE DURRELL: G. S. Fraser
T. S. ELIOT: M. C. Bradbrook
T. S. ELIOT: The Making of 'The
Waste Land': M. C. Bradbrook
FORD MADOX FORD:
Kenneth Young
FORSTER: Rex Warner
FRY: Derek Stanford
GALSWORTHY: R. H. Mottram
GOLDING: Stephen Medcalf
GRAVES: M. Seymour-Smith
GRAHAM GREENE:
Francis Wyndham
HARTLEY: Paul Bloomfield
A. E. HOUSMAN: Ian Scott-Kilvert
TED HUGHES: Keith Sagar
ALDOUS HUXLEY: Jocelyn Brooke
ISHERWOOD: Francis King
HENRY JAMES: Michael Swan
HANSFORD JOHNSON: Isabel Quigly
JOYCE: J. I. M. Stewart
KIPLING: Bonamy Dobrée
LARKIN: Alan Brownjohn
D. H. LAWRENCE: Kenneth Young
D. H. LAWRENCE I:
J. F. C. Littlewood
LESSING: Michael Thorpe
C. DAY LEWIS: Clifford Dyment
WYNDHAM LEWIS:
E. W. F. Tomlin
MACDIARMID: Edwin Morgan
MACKENZIE: K. Young
MACNEICE: John Press
MANSFIELD: Ian Gordon

MASEFIELD: L. A. G. Strong
MAUGHAM: J. Brophy
GEORGE MOORE:
A. Norman Jeffares
MURDOCH: A. S. Byatt
NAIPAUL: Michael Thorpe
NARAYAN: William Walsh
NEWBY: G. S. Fraser
O'CASEY: W. A. Armstrong
ORWELL: Tom Hopkinson
OSBORNE: Simon Trussler
OWEN: Dominic Hibberd
PINTER: John Russell Taylor
POETS OF THE 1939-45 WAR:
R. N. Currey
POWELL: Bernard Bergonzi
POWYS BROTHERS: R. C. Churchill
PRIESTLEY: Ivor Brown
PROSE WRITERS OF WORLD WAR I:
M. S. Greicus
HERBERT READ: Francis Berry
SHAFFER: John Russell Taylor
SHAW: A. C. Ward
EDITH SITWELL: John Lehmann
SNOW: William Cooper
SPARK: Patricia Stubbs
STOPPARD: C. W. E. Bigsby
STOREY: John Russell Taylor
SYNGE & LADY GREGORY:
E. Coxhead
DYLAN THOMAS: G. S. Fraser
G. M. TREVELYAN: J. H. Plumb
WAR POETS: 1914-18:
E. Blunden
EVELYN WAUGH:
Christopher Hollis
WELLS: Kenneth Young
WESKER: Glenda Leeming
PATRICK WHITE: R. F. Brissenden
ANGUS WILSON: K. W. Gransden
VIRGINIA WOOLF: B. Blackstone
YEATS: G. S. Fraser